teach me about
Traveling

Written by Joy Berry
Illustrated by Bartholomew

Published by
Peter Pan Industries
Newark, NJ 07105

Printed in the United States of America

ISBN: 0-88149-708-8

Publisher: Peter Pan Industries, Newark, NJ 07105
Producer: Marilyn Berry
Editor: Orly Kelly
Consultant: Kathy McBride
Design and production: Abigail Johnston
Art Direction: Rob Lavery
Graphic coordination: Filip Associates, Inc.

Sometimes it is fun

to go away from home.

I get ready to go.

I get dressed.

I go to the bathroom.

I get the things

I want to take with me.

I take my sweater or jacket.

I take my favorite blanket or toy.

I take something to do.

I do not want my hands or feet

to get closed in the car door.

I am careful

when I get into the car.

I keep my hands and feet

away from the door.

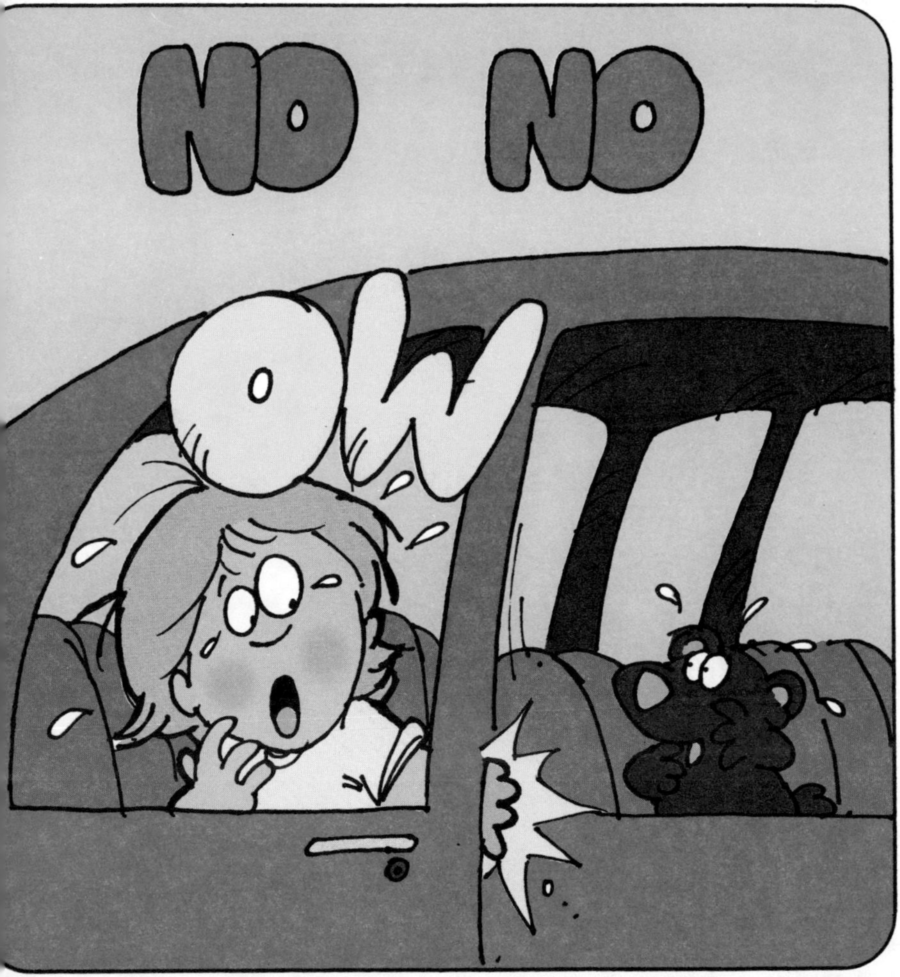
NO NO
OW

I do not want to get hurt.

I get into my car seat.

I fasten my safety belt.

I stay in my car seat

while I am in the car.

I do not want my hands

to get caught in the window.

I do not roll the window

up or down.

I do not want to fall out of the car.

I do not unlock the car door.

I do not touch the door handle.

I do not get out of the car

until it is parked.

I do not want the car to crash.

The person driving the car

must think about driving.

I do nothing that would bother

the person driving the car.

I do not want to lose anything.

I do not throw anything

out of the car window.

I do not want to get lost.

I do not go anywhere by myself.

I always stay with the person

who is taking care of me.

Sometimes I ride in

a shopping cart.

I do not want to

fall out of the cart.

I sit down in the shopping cart.

I do not want anything

to fall on me.

I do not reach for things

that are outside the shoppping cart.

Sometimes I eat away from home.

I sit in a high chair or

booster chair.

I do not want to fall.

I sit carefully in the chair.

Sometimes I sleep

away from home.

I miss my house.

I miss my bed.

I remember that I will be

home soon.

Then I do not feel so bad.

It is fun to go away.

It is also fun to come back home.

I am careful

so I can come back home safely.

helpful hints for parents about
Traveling

Dear Parents:

The purpose of this book is—

    to show children how to prepare for travel, and

    to teach children what they need to do to remain safe and
    well while they are traveling.

You can best implement the purpose of this book by—

    reading it to your child, and

    reading the following *Helpful Hints* and using them
    whenever applicable.

TRAVEL SAFETY

Safety procedures for travel include:
- Provide a safety-tested and approved car seat for your child.
- Have your baby's car seat ready for the first ride home from the hospital.
- Pad and cover your car seat and infant carrier with an absorbent material such as terry cloth.
- Always use the restraining belts in both car seats and infant carriers.
- Never leave your child unattended in a car seat or infant carrier.

TRAVELING SUPPLIES

Suggested items to keep in your car:
- A washable or disposable changing surface. Plastic garbage bags work well and can be used for diaper disposal.
- Premoistened towelettes for easy cleanup.
- Ointment or powder for diaper rash.
- A minimum of two disposable diapers.
- Plastic bags for used diapers.
- Eating and drinking utensils, including a plastic baby bottle, spoon, and cup.
- a bib.
- Sealed containers of fruit juice and baby food.
- Protective clothing such as a sweater, a jacket, a warm hat, or a sun hat.
- A full change of clothing.

- One or more baby blankets.
- Small toys and security objects.

Keep these items in a box or bag and replace them as they are used.

Suggested medical supplies to take when you travel with your child:

- vitamins
- thermometer
- baby aspirin
- diaper rash ointment
- medicine for diarrhea
- antihistamines for colds or allergies
- glycerine suppositories for constipation
- sunscreen lotion
- vital information such as your doctor's phone number, medical insurance card or number, and a health information book.

All medications should be in child-proof containers. Keep important medications with you. Do not put them in baggage that might be lost or stolen.

EQUIPMENT NEEDED AWAY FROM HOME

Take only what you and your child will need when you travel. Many of the necessities can be borrowed or rented when you reach your destination. You may want to call ahead to reserve them.

Here are some items your child will most likely need while away from home:

- a car seat.
- a portable potty. This is especially good for long car trips.
- A bed.
- A playpen. This can also be used as a bed.
- A standard or portable highchair. A portable one can be attached to a table top. (Most restaurants supply highchairs.)
- A walker. This can be used in place of a highchair.
- A stroller.
- An infant seat.
- A baby carrier.

When your child sleeps away from home, you can create an instant bed from one of the following:

- A dresser drawer that has been removed from the dresser (for small infants only).
- Covered foam padding.
- A playpen mat.
- An inflatable wading pool. (This can also be used as a bathtub or playpen.)

These beds should be placed on the floor in an area that is safe and free of drafts. Be sure to provide enough padding to make the bed comfortable.

FOOD AND BEVERAGES FOR TRAVEL

Bottles

Procedures for keeping bottles cold:

- Put six bottles in a six-pack container and place the container in a six-pack ice chest.
- Wrap the bottle in a small towel or diaper, then pack it in ice cubes in a sealable plastic bag.

Procedures for warming bottles and keeping them warm:

- Fill a plastic container with hot water and place the bottle in the water. The contents should be warm in three to six minutes.
- Run the hot tap water over the bottle until the contents are warm.
- Wrap the warm bottle in a dry washcloth. Place it in an empty tennis ball can and snap on the plastic lid.

Beverages

Here are some suggestions for preparing beverages for travel:

- Premeasure powdered formula and put it into a sealable plastic bag. Add warm water from a thermos bottle when your baby is ready to eat.
- Prewarm canned formula and carry it in a thermos bottle.
- Carry a large thermos jug of cold water and plastic cups with handles. Water from home is less likely to cause digestive problems.
- Add premeasured servings of hot cocoa mix to hot water from a a thermos bottle when traveling in cold weather.
- Freeze sealed containers of juice before your trip. Allow the beverages to defrost en route.